CONTENTS

Published 2024. Little Brother Books Ltd, Ground Floor, 23 Southernhay East, Exeter, Devon EX1 1QL
books@littlebrotherbooks.co.uk | www.littlebrotherbooks.co.uk
Printed in the United Kingdom.
The Little Brother Books trademark, email and website addresses, are the sole and exclusive properties of Little Brother Books Limited.

ONLINE ACTIVITIES

On some of the pages you will see QR codes. These QR codes take you to online Purple Mash activities which support learning from the relevant page.

To use the QR codes, scan the QR code with the camera on your web enabled tablet, click on the link and the activity will appear on screen.

Alternatively, QR readers are available on the app store for your device.

SCAN CODE

purple mash

PARTS OF A SENTENCE

Each part of Wallace's latest invention has a particular function, just like in a sentence where words have specific functions.

Words in a sentence will belong to particular groups called word classes. You will know them as **nouns**, **verbs**, **adjectives** etc. Each one of these has a different role.

1

Match the type of word to its job.

noun	**a.** Describes a noun or a pronoun.
verb	**b.** Always used just before a noun that gives more information about it.
adjective	**c.** Joins phrases, clauses and sentences.
adverb	**d.** The name of a person, object, time or place.
conjunction	**e.** Shows more about the time, position or direction of the action.
pronoun	**f.** Describes an action, thought or state of being.
determiner	**g.** Mostly describes verbs but also adjectives and other adverbs.
preposition	**h.** Used to replace a noun to prevent repeating it over and over.

2

Look at the words below. Can you sort them into the correct word class?

Wallace	under	he	as	because
inventive	think	clever	quickly	run
trousers	some	him	near	and
is	West Wallaby Street	the	friend	suspiciously

noun	verb	adjective	adverb

conjunction	pronoun	determiner	preposition

LINKING IDEAS WITHIN A PARAGRAPH

Wallace is writing a report on how much bread they sold this week to show Gromit that he is being organised.

1 Here are the notes that Wallace took while making his report. Can you help him write the report by writing the steps into full sentences using the time conjunctions and adverbial phrases to help make the report flow better? Remember to put a comma after time conjunctions and adverbial phrases when they're at the start of a sentence.

Time conjunctions:
next, later, after, then, first, finally, when, until, meanwhile, initially, immediately, eventually, afterwards.

Adverbial phrases:
once completed, at this point, after a while, to begin with, ten minutes later, soon after, a few minutes later.

WALLACE'S EXPERIMENT NOTES:

- Noticed that Gromit is making more loaves than usual – Gromit had to spend more time making recipes and spent hardly any time doing anything else; Gromit is always sleepy because he's working more hours than ever.

- Discovered a way of mixing ingredients that saves time, and It works really well.

- So many orders came in one day, that Gromit could not keep up with them all. Must help him keep on top of them all.

- Noticed we are running low on flour, and Gromit needs to put in a new order for more.

USEFUL WORDS TO SPELL – PART I

Wendolene Ramsbottom is seeing double! She has noticed that in her knitting patterns, lots of words that she is reading have double letters. Some even have two sets of double letters. Knowing how many double letters there are can help her to learn the words.

1

Help Wendolene find and circle all the words that contain double letters.

accommodate	accompany	according	achieve
aggressive	amateur	ancient	apparent
appreciate	attached	available	average
awkward	bargain	bruise	category
cemetery	committee	communicate	community
competition	conscience	conscious	controversy
convenience	correspond	criticise	curiosity

2

Can you find the words with double letters in the wordsearch below?

w	c	c	x	l	u	z	k	a	d	a	a	s	q	c	a	i	a
d	o	a	n	m	x	w	m	p	i	p	c	i	c	o	y	a	k
l	m	c	q	d	c	a	d	p	y	p	c	k	o	r	z	g	y
p	m	c	p	c	j	c	a	r	s	a	o	y	m	r	r	g	r
c	u	o	n	m	l	c	t	e	n	r	m	q	m	e	f	r	y
e	n	r	y	y	l	o	t	c	i	e	m	a	u	s	m	e	e
x	i	d	x	b	j	m	a	i	w	n	o	f	n	p	w	s	p
o	c	i	i	w	d	p	c	a	s	t	d	f	i	o	x	s	q
t	a	n	l	h	m	a	h	t	k	s	a	u	t	n	u	i	w
r	t	g	k	c	s	n	e	e	a	x	t	i	y	d	c	v	x
v	e	a	i	o	r	y	d	y	w	z	e	f	x	i	t	e	b
g	z	t	a	u	f	b	a	c	o	m	m	i	t	t	e	e	s

COMMAS, BRACKETS AND DASHES

When adding extra details to sentences, you can use commas, brackets or dashes to mark where the words and phrases (known as parenthesis) have been added.

Brackets are used more for facts and figures and in formal writing. **Dashes** are often used more informally. One way of adding extra information is by including extra facts about the person, place or object.

90°

1

Wallace is planning to decorate his house and create a photo wall. He's put lots of information into his plan for where each photo should be placed. Fill in the gaps in Wallace's plan using the information in the box below.

a. It is important to get the right height, _____ _____, so everyone can be seen in the frames.

b. Gromit (_____) should always be next to Wallace wherever possible.

c. Beware placing pictures of Gromit next to Piella Bakewell - _____ - or he might not be very happy.

d. Fluffles (_____) likes the limelight, so don't put a picture in front of her.

e. It is best to be placed next to me, _____, as I am very photogenic.

> also known as the sweet spot
>
> the expert baker
>
> the rival bakery owner
>
> the pampered pooch
>
> the handsome inventor

2

Gromit has packed the sentences below full of information but has forgotten to use parenthesis. Choose whether to use commas, brackets or dashes for each sentence and mark where they should go.

a. West Wallaby Street founded in the 1600s is located 'Up North' in Lancashire.

b. It has a large population approximately 20,000 residents and has beautiful parks.

c. The two cities found nearby within a 60 mile radius are Preston and Chorley.

d. There are lots of restaurants including The Cheese Club and Bake-O-Lite's bakery serving a wide range of cuisine.

SPEEDY READING

Wallace and Gromit are taking part in a football match. Skim read the report to find the vital match statistics.

THE SOCCAMATIC SENSATION!

It was a dramatic night at the stadium as Wallace and Gromit seized victory in the cup final, after a nail-biting match against their rivals!

The enthusiastic crowd were right behind Wallace in the first half as the ball bounced across the pitch, chased by two teams determined to win the match.

Gromit, as always, was a clear contender in the battle against the opposition; his kick so forceful that the ball burst! The other side got the ball extremely close to the goal in their first three attacks. However, Wallace and Gromit fought back, nearly matching the rival team's attempts at goal by unleashing the Soccamatic.

There was huge excitement when the rivals were close to the goal, prompting an outbreak of rapturous applause from the fans. As the first set of balls were fired by the Soccamatic, Wallace was able to move in to the rival's penalty area where he was close to scoring a goal.

After some entertainment during the half-time break, it was back to business in the second half! With the two teams neck and neck, Wallace was able to fire the Soccamatic balls into the goal, to the dismay of the other team.

The rival team from over the border should never be discounted, and they fought strong and hard in the final few minutes of the game. However, the crowd applauded Wallace and Gromit for their victory and a cracking game of football!

1 Complete the table by deciding whether the statements below are true or false.

	TRUE	FALSE
a. The rival team burst the football.		
b. Fans broke into rapturous applause when the ball is close to the goal.		
c. The rival team is from the next village.		
d. Wallace and Gromit won by using the Soccamatic.		
e. Wallace and Gromit were applauded for their victory.		

2 Why was the game so important? _____

ADDING SUFFIXES TO CREATE VERBS

Piella Bakewell loves dark and dramatic action words. She is writing a journal entry about her hatred for bakers!

You can create verbs from nouns and adjectives by adding **suffixes**. Remember that adding a **suffix** can cause the spelling of the root word to change.

1

Help Piella Bakewell create some dramatic verbs about her hatred of bakers by using the correct suffixes. Choose from the suffixes below. You may need to take off an existing word ending to add the suffix on.

-ate	-en	-ify	-ise

a. horror ➡ _____

b. threat ➡ _____

c. fright ➡ _____

d. terror ➡ _____

e. energy ➡ _____

f. irritation ➡ _____

g. Which word can create two verbs?

_____

2

Piella is changing these words using the same suffixes.
Can you write the new word using the correct suffix from the ones above?
You may need to remove a word ending before adding a new one.

beautiful _____

character _____

hard _____

active _____

electric _____

light _____

regular _____

equal _____

SUFFIXES -ABLE AND -ABLY

Top Bun bakery products are great for baking all kinds of treats. Wallace is writing an advert for his baking products and is trying to use the suffix -able and -ably as much as possible to describe them.

To decide whether to use the suffixes **-able** or **-ible**, you can follow these rules: If there is a complete root word without the suffix then add **-able**. If there is not, it is spelt with **-ible**.

horror → horr → horrible   honor → honorable

Not a full word   Is a full word

Words that end in: **-ation** use **-able**. Words that end in **-ce** and **-ge** keep the **e** before the suffix **-able**. This also applies to **-ably** and **-ibly**.

1

Write the correct **-able** or **-ably** word in the descriptions. Hint: There is one exception here that uses **-ible**. The first one has been done for you.

a. Wallace is quite ____adorable____. (adoration)

b. He has _____ talents. (consider)

c. His products are always _____. (depend)

d. In the kitchen, Gromit is highly _____. (response)

e. You will view the work _____. (favour)

f. The whole experience will be _____. (enjoy)

g. He is always honest and _____. (rely)

h. He is very _____. (knowledge)

2

Wallace has written his own anti-advert for rival bakery Bake-O-Lite. He has used lots of words that end **-ce** and **-ge**, what is the rule for these?

a. Bake-O-Lite is also very _____. (change)

b. Their excess waste is barely _____. (manage)

c. The flavour is often not _____. (notice)

MAKING AN ACCOUNT FLOW ACROSS PARAGRAPHS

Wallace is trying to write a story about his invention trials with Gromit. He's made some notes to help him.

You can make a story flow by linking paragraphs using different methods:

Use an ellipsis: These are three dots in sequence at the end of a sentence like this …

Repeat words that you want to emphasise between paragraphs. For example, if you are trying to convey a feeling of beauty, you might use the word beauty several times across paragraphs adding suffixes when necessary for variety.

Repeat phrases the same way. For example, a spooky tale might repeat the phrase 'the darkest of nights,' several times.

1 Can you write his notes into sentences and add extra details? Make sure you use repeating words and phrases across the paragraphs and finish each paragraph on an ellipsis.

NOTES:

Paragraph 1:
- Had idea, Wallace sketched them out.
- Gromit tried out invention, it failed.
- Was hit accidentally in the face with the punch-o-tron bag.

Paragraph 2:
- Tried again the next day.
- Safety lock failed.
- Wallace supervising.
- Tripped over punch-o-tron's hand.

Paragraph 3:
- Final attempt.
- Punch-o-tron won't stop punching.
- Exhausted – Wallace called Gromit for help.

SEMICOLONS, COLONS AND DASHES

Wallace loves cheese and often writes about his love for it! Today he is writing about his favourite cheeses!

30°

Colons join dependent clauses **:** The parts before and after the colon are full sentences on their own but the second part adds more detail to the first.

Semicolons extend a sentence by joining together two independent clauses **;** they do not need to be full sentences on their own.

If you want to emphasise a section — use **dashes** — this makes it stand out.

1

Can you match these related parts of a sentence together and write them below with a colon in the middle?

a. Cheddar cheese is made in the village of Cheddar.

b. Wallace visited Cheddar on a cheese pilgrimage.

He had to go there as he had run out of supplies.

It's one of Wallace's favourite cheeses!

_____

_____

_____

2

In this sentence, replace the underlined word with appropriate punctuation to join the two clauses.

Wallace drove out of town <u>because</u> he was in search of much needed crackers.

3

Separate the clauses in this sentence using dashes to see how this creates emphasis and drama.

In the end, Wallace stayed in town and opened a cheese shop, gaining the respect of the community, where his cheese was loved by many.

READING COMPREHENSION: INFERENCE PART I

Wallace and Gromit are visiting a library to research ideas for new inventions. Use inference to think about what the writing is hinting at and find evidence to answer the questions.

Cautiously, Wallace and Gromit picked their way through the library's heap of electronics manuals. Dusty old books surrounded them; only the dimly lit bulb gave them light as they searched for the next invention idea.

The hushed sounds of the pages turning were suddenly silenced as Gromit fell upon the perfect idea.

Out of nowhere, the words started dancing across the page.

The duo paused in shock as they gazed at the enormous list of instructions and the strange picture of the finished invention. It was a sock collector: that much was evident from the sticky claw, the numerous holders, and the sheer physical size of the contraption. The collector's hands whirred at high speed as the contraption collected socks lost, and found, from all kinds of places.

Wallace, in all his years of inventing, had never seen anything like it before.

"Wow, this is incredible." He breathed, gazing down in awe and wonder. Of great interest, was the source of the energy needed for the invention.

"Look at that," Wallace gasped, his eyes wide. "It's powered by a bio battery! We have to get one."

1

Gromit needs help answering these questions. Can you find hints in the text to help him answer them?

a. What suggests the library was peaceful before Wallace and Gromit found the book?

_____

b. Wallace "breathed, gazing down in awe and wonder". What does this suggest about how he is feeling?

- [ ] He is surprised by what he sees.
- [ ] He is terrified by what he sees.
- [ ] He is amazed by what he sees.
- [ ] He is saddened by what he sees.

2

Can you find some supporting evidence in the text to answer these questions?

a. Find a piece of evidence to suggest that the library is dark.

_____

_____

b. How does Wallace feel when he discovers the bio battery? How do you know?

_____

_____

ADDING PREFIXES

In Wallace's house, inventions often go haywire when the blueprints are not followed correctly.

Prefixes can be used to change the meaning of words. The prefixes below make many words have the opposite meaning.

dis-	de-	mis-	over-	re-	un-

Look at this example:

Appear is a verb; it means something comes into sight or becomes visible.
For example, Gromit suddenly **appeared** in the basement lab.

Disappear means cease to be visible: The prefix **dis-** has changed the meaning of the verb. For example, Gromit seemed to **disappear** from the room.

1

This is Piella's journal entry about Gromit:

However, Bob the baker has seen an opportunity for mischief, he has intercepted the diary and added prefixes to make the words mean the opposite of what Piella meant.

Insert some prefixes from the choices above to make Piella's diary entry change in meaning.

Fluffles always _____ behaves. She usually _____ agrees with everything that I suggest. I strongly _____ approve of her _____ obedience and her _____ reaction to any suggestion. I enjoyed the opportunity to _____ view the way Fluffles _____ acted when given a challenge. She is very _____ respectful and makes everyone feel very _____ comfortable.

2

Bob the Baker was caught and has been given a list of chores he has to do for Piella to make it up to her.

Use the correct prefix either **re-** or **over-** so the list makes sense.

a. • _____ take managing the washing up after dinner.

b. • _____ build Piella a huge mansion.

c. • _____ write the diary entry correctly... 100 times!

d. • Promise to _____ look any mischievous opportunities for the next two weeks.

e. • Give Piella a massage to ____ charge her damaged pride.

f. • _____ make Piella's bed every morning for a week.

SPELLINGS: EI WORDS PART I

Wendolene Ramsbottom is used to following rules because of all the instructions she needs to read for her knitting patterns. She's just learnt a new rule for how to spell words with 'ei' in them: i before e except after c. This rule only works when the 'ei' makes the 'ee' sound.

1

See how quickly you can reach the finish in this game. Roll a dice and move the number of spaces thrown. If you land on a word that's spelt incorrectly, go back to the start and try again.

START	conceive	reciept	conceit	recieve

FINISH	deceit	decieve	cieling	perceive

2

Wendolene wants to make a tricky version of the game above with some irregular **ei** and **ie** words, but first she needs to know how to spell them. Can you spot which of the words below follow the rule and which are exceptions? Finish spelling the words correctly.

	a.			d.	
	prot__n	ei / ie		f___ld	ei / ie
	b.			e.	
	shr__k	ei / ie		caff___ne	ei / ie
	c.			f.	
	s__ze	ei / ie		th__f	ei / ie

13

WRITING A PLAYSCRIPT

The newspaper reporter from the 'Daily Beagle' has been observing the comings and goings of West Wallaby Street. They now wish to turn their comic strip about them into a playscript.

A playscript should contain the following:
List of actors, setting, actor name followed by the line they say with a new line for each speaker, stage directions written on a new line and in brackets. Reading it should help you visualise the action in your head. Here is an example:

Actors: Wallace (genius inventor), Gromit (canine sidekick) and Wendolene Ramsbottom (keen knitter)

Setting: Wallace's house

Wallace: (picks up the telephone receiver) Hello? Wallace and Gromit's wash 'n' go window cleaning service! May we be of assistance?

Wendolene: (sounds nervous) Hello? Yes, my windows can do with a jolly good clean. The Wool Shop in the High Street. Soon as you can!

(Wallace gives Gromit the thumbs-up sign.)

1

The newspaper's latest comic strip starts after Feathers McGraw tries to make a getaway, and Wallace tries to catch him. Follow the rules above to turn the comic strip into a playscript. Write your script on a piece of paper.

Let the getaway begin!

You won't catch me!

Don't worry Gromit, I'm right behind you.

Leave it to me! I'll get the bounder.

WRITING A NEWSPAPER REPORT

There has been great public interest in Wallace's latest invention: his new porridge gun which can shoot porridge at high speeds. Here are the journalist's notes from an interview with Wallace.

1

Use the notes to write a report. Think of a suitable headline and ensure that your writing captures the excitement of the event while including the facts. It should include:

- **Who? Wallace**
- **Where? 62 West Wallaby Street**
- **When? Last week**
- **What? Created a new and improved way to eat porridge**
- **How? Made a Porridge gun**

Write in the third person: like an outsider looking in, using pronouns like 'he', 'she', 'it' or 'they'.

Use time conjunctions such as 'firstly', 'meanwhile', 'later', 'finally' and 'eventually' to help create cohesion.

- Wanted to find a quicker way to eat porridge.
- Started researching for different methods.
- Found an old Scottish manuscript for using a slingshot to eat porridge quickly.
- Used the manuscript to make the slingshot.
- Realised that he could improve on his invention by making it faster.
- Designed a new porridge slingshot.
- Renamed it to the Porridge Gun.
- Tested it by himself and with Gromit.
- Gave it to the general public to use.
- The general public loved it and wanted to buy more for their friends and family.
- He gave the blueprint out for a small fee so everyone could enjoy his invention.

RELATIVE CLAUSES

Piella Bakewell likes to write a journal and updates it every day. Can you help her extend her sentences using relative clauses?

1

Relative clauses add more information about a noun in a sentence. Complete the sentences below by adding one of these relative pronouns in each gap:

which	where	when	whose	that

a. The bakery is coming up to a very busy time, _____ there is no end to the number of orders.

b. There are confused customers in the shop, _____ orders are incorrect.

c. All of a sudden, the clock, _____ is big and shiny, strikes one and it's time to bake again.

d. The waiting customers comment on the delicious aroma, _____ wafts out of the kitchen.

2

Piella has decided to write a poem in this section of her journal. Can you rewrite each sentence below and add a relative clause using a relative pronoun about the word in bold? Remember to put commas around the relative clause if it is in the middle of the sentence.
The first one has been done for you.

a. Dancing, prancing in the carrot cake **maze**,

whose walls were higher than any gaze.

b. The **bakers** joining full of glee and song

_____

c. A **shadowy figure** appeared later that night

_____

d. The whisps of icing sugar chilled the **ground**

_____

SPELLINGS: EI WORDS PART 2

Wendolene has been working hard on her tricky 'ei' spelling game, but Wallace has walked past and spilled tea all over the answer cards, making some of the words dissolve.

1

Tick the cards that have the correct spelling. Put a cross on the cards that are spelt incorrectly and write the correct letters in the gaps. To help you, use the rule: i before e except after c. Remember, this rule only works when the 'ei' makes the sound 'ee'.

a.
Word shown:
perceive

Correct or incorrect
☐

Correct spelling:
pe_ _ _ _ _ _e

b.
Word shown:
recieve

Correct or incorrect
☐

Correct spelling:
re_ _ _ _ _e

c.
Word shown:
nieghbour

Correct or incorrect
☐

Correct spelling:
n_ _ _ _ _bour

d.
Word shown:
field

Correct or incorrect
☐

Correct spelling:
f_ _ _d

e.
Word shown:
theif

Correct or incorrect
☐

Correct spelling:
th_ _f

f.
Word shown:
ancient

Correct or incorrect
☐

Correct spelling:
a_ _ _ _ _nt

g.
Word shown:
reciept

Correct or incorrect
☐

Correct spelling:
re_ _ _pt

h.
Word shown:
leisure

Correct or incorrect
☐

Correct spelling:
l_ _ _ _ _re

2

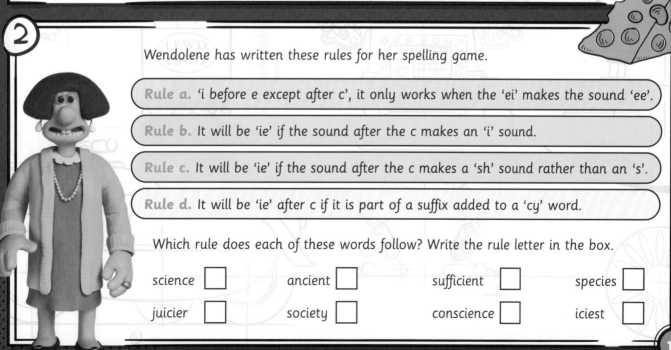

Wendolene has written these rules for her spelling game.

Rule a. 'i before e except after c', it only works when the 'ei' makes the sound 'ee'.

Rule b. It will be 'ie' if the sound after the c makes an 'i' sound.

Rule c. It will be 'ie' if the sound after the c makes a 'sh' sound rather than an 's'.

Rule d. It will be 'ie' after c if it is part of a suffix added to a 'cy' word.

Which rule does each of these words follow? Write the rule letter in the box.

science ☐   ancient ☐   sufficient ☐   species ☐

juicier ☐   society ☐   conscience ☐   iciest ☐

COLONS AND SEMICOLONS IN LISTS

Wallace is trying to be more organised so he's learning how to write lists correctly. He's found out he needs to use a colon at the start of a list and then commas or semicolons depending on the size of the item in the list.

Example:

Short items
Items to pack in my van: pen, pencil, extra fuel, cheese, crossword.

Long items
Today's tasks: Gromit will wash up; Wallace will buy cheese; Gromit will check ingredients;

1 Wallace always has a plan. There is a science fair coming up and he is determined to get top prize. He has made some lists to help organise himself. The lists should use commas as the items are short: Punctuate his lists correctly.

a. Things Gromit needs wire screwdriver paint

b. Items to source wood nails saw bicarbonate of soda.

c. The days I can submit my project Monday Tuesday Wednesday Thursday Friday.

2 Gromit is putting the finishing touches to his plan to secure the winning prize for best monoplane pilot, and he has made a list to help him decide what to do. He needs to use semicolons between the items as they are longer and contain commas. Can you check he has included all the semicolons needed and add any that he has missed out?

To get the winning prize and not crash, I need to: fill the fuel tank with enough fuel to fly for a long distance and fast; show the other pilots that I have won many other competitions to scare them, even though I have only won two put cheese in the other planes jets to make them spin slower get Wallace to hack the other planes to do their tricks wrong; do five loop-the-loops.

READING COMPREHENSION: VOCABULARY

Wallace is researching recipes for the Autochef. He knows understanding the mix of ingredients is important, so if he's stuck on a word, he tries to use another word in its place. If the sentence still makes sense, he's found a word with the same meaning (synonym) to help him understand the text.

The perfect recipe

Many bakers experience a satisfying feeling when they come across the perfect mix for tinned loaves, sticky buns or sweet cakes. The most dedicated of bakers know no bounds when it comes to sourcing the perfect ingredients. Conversely, if the mix is not quite right, the recipes can go very wrong.

Why does this happen?

Due to the ratios of ingredients, and the temperature of the ovens, without a perfect balance, it can cause an error to occur. Recipes are similar, but small increments or temperature changes can cause big fluctuations in the recipe and can cause the most extreme results.

If the temperature is too cool, the bread will fail to rise. However, if it's too hot, the bread will instantly burn, but it could remain uncooked in the middle.

1

Wallace is identifying some of the key vocabulary in the article. Can you help him by answering the following questions?

a. Find and copy a word that means looking for, or finding. _____

b. Find and copy a phrase that explains what causes big fluctuations in the recipe.

_____

c. Find and copy a word that means, fairly like each other. _____

2

Wallace is having trouble understanding the end of the text. Can you help? Look at the final sentence. Which of these words or phrases is closest in meaning to 'instantly'?

☐ In due course   ☐ Soon

☐ Straight away   ☐ Quickly

3

Wallace is trying to explain what one of the words means. Can you help him write the answer? Look at the sentence beginning, 'Conversely, if the mix is not quite right...' What does the word conversely mean?

_____

ADVERBS TO INDICATE POSSIBILITY

Piella would say her chances of winning any competitive event are a certainty. She feels she has no use for any other adverbs that describe how likely something is to happen!

1

Separate the adverbs in the box into those which show that Piella is **certain** or *very* **likely** to win and those which show it **might** happen.

Certain or very likely	Might

certainly
definitely
maybe
possibly
clearly
perhaps
probably
obviously

2

Look at the sentences below. Circle the correct adverb to complete the sentences to help Piella work out her chances of impressing investors in next week's Bake-O-Lite meeting.

a. As it is in December, the meeting will be in the bakery next to the ovens, so it will **maybe/clearly** be nice and warm.

b. The investors are very intimidating so it will **definitely/ possibly** be a challenging and nerve-wracking meeting.

c. Piella is concerned that if she makes a mistake, she might **certainly/perhaps** lose the investors trust.

d. The investors are quite particular, so if Piella makes a maths mistake, they could **possibly/obviously** decide to invest elsewhere.

SPELLINGS: HOMOPHONES

Wallace and Gromit know all too well that things can sound the same and look different! The trick is to know the meaning of each word to help know when to use it.

1

Wallace has spotted that these homophones are spelt differently when they are a noun (the name) or a verb (the action). Nouns are spelt with a **c** and verbs are spelt with an **s**. Help her put the nouns and verbs in the correct column.

Noun	Verb

advice/advise

devise/device

license/licence

practice/practise

prophesy/prophecy

Complete these sentences with the correct homophone.

advice/advise
devise/device
practice/practise

a. Wallace asked Gromit for _____ about the best way to make cheese. Gromit tried to _____ him that practice was important.

b. Feathers McGraw tried to _____ a plan to steal to remote control _____.

c. Gromit delivered bread to the medical _____ to cheer up the patients. He had to _____ the recipe every day to perfect the loaves.

2

Wallace is trying to match these homophones to the correct definition. Can you help him match them correctly?

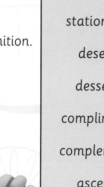

stationary

stationery

desert

dessert

compliment

complement

ascent

assent

to abandon, a barren place

agreement, to agree

to make something complete or more complete

paper, envelopes etc.

going up

not moving

paper, envelopes etc.

a sweet course after the main course of a meal

A20g

WALLACE
62 WEST WALLABY ST

HANDWRITING PRACTICE – PART 1

Wallace takes pride in his handwriting. He joins letters and makes sure that the spacing and sizing is always perfect.

1

Copy the sentences Wallace is practising.

Neat handwriting helps you make better plans.

Practise makes perfect with handwriting.

2

Wallace has written a plan for Gromit. Can you copy it out neatly?

To win the cheese making competition, we will need to get the best recipe. We could keep it a secret from everyone else. We could swoop in at the last minute, with a show-stopping entry.

CREATIVE WRITING: WRITING A PLOT

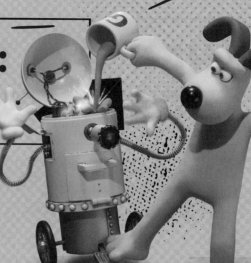

You now know so much about Wallace & Gromit, you've been given the job of writing the plot for an episode! Remember to include the reactions of all the characters to a situation and think about what they would all do.

1

Use these ideas to get you started or use one of your own.

Wallace is always creating experiments and inventions to try to help his friends and family. In this episode, Wallace has decided to help one of his friends with their problem by creating an experiment or an invention.
- Choose which problem you think he should solve.
- How could he solve it?
- What happens when he tells the friend he is going to help?
- How does the experiment or invention work? (Or maybe it doesn't work!)
- What happens after?
- Remember to include the friend's reactions!

Wallace has run out of cheese and wants to know how he can easily make more.

Wallace is trying to create new inventions but keeps forgetting what he was creating in the middle of each design.

Wendolene is frustrated because the yarn in her wool balls are tangled and keep breaking when she's trying to knit.

VERB TENSES

Different tenses are used when describing something that happened either in the past, present or future.

The present perfect tense is a way to show that an action started in the past but not at a specific time. For example, Wallace has eaten cheese with Gromit 3256 times.

1

Wallace, Gromit and their friends have had a busy day. Write a sentence for each of them using the present perfect tense ('has') and the past tense of the verb. The first one has been done for you.

Read inventor magazine.	Fix a broken invention.	Wait for bread to be baked.	Walk into the wool shop.	Eat a bowl of dog food.

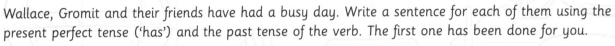

a. Wallace	**b.** Gromit	**c.** Piella	**d.** Wendolene	**e.** Preston
Wallace has read the inventor magazine.				

2

Wallace is trying to convert these simple past tense sentences into past perfect tense sentences. Gromit has explained that he needs to add 'had' before the verb and check the verb is in the correct past tense form. Can you help him change the sentences to past perfect tense? The first one has been done for you.

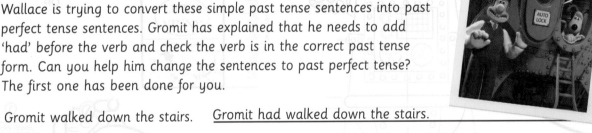

a. Gromit walked down the stairs. Gromit had walked down the stairs.

b. He noticed my invention. _____

c. He tripped on it anyway. _____

d. He landed in a pile of wires. _____

e. Gromit tidied everything away neatly. _____

USEFUL WORDS TO SPELL – PART 2

Sometimes, Gromit just likes the quiet life!

He has noticed that some of the words in the list below have silent letters or do not sound the way they are written. Sounding the words out and stressing the tricky parts the way they are written can help to learn these words, e.g. envi-RON-ment, de-FI-NITE.

1

Read through the words in the table then search for them in the word search. The words can be going downwards, left to right, or diagonal.

definite	desperate	determined	develop
dictionary	disastrous	embarrass	environment
equip	especially	explanation	exaggerate
excellent	existence	familiar	foreign
frequently	government	guarantee	hindrance

d	e	l	f	g	t	k	i	e	q	m	f	o	c	e	s	y	e
i	x	d	c	f	a	m	i	l	i	a	r	e	e	x	d	s	n
s	p	k	e	z	o	b	o	d	v	t	e	x	x	c	i	d	v
a	l	d	m	t	i	r	w	e	k	i	q	i	a	e	c	e	i
s	a	e	b	a	e	g	e	f	m	b	u	s	g	l	t	s	r
t	n	v	a	g	b	r	z	i	y	z	e	t	g	l	i	p	o
r	a	e	r	u	i	e	m	n	g	k	n	e	e	e	o	e	n
o	t	l	r	a	n	q	s	i	j	n	t	n	r	n	n	r	m
u	i	o	a	r	i	u	c	t	n	t	l	c	a	t	a	a	e
s	o	p	s	a	d	i	l	e	n	e	y	e	t	t	r	t	n
v	n	t	s	n	p	p	u	k	y	i	d	y	e	v	y	e	t
j	s	l	v	t	e	s	p	e	c	i	a	l	l	y	q	e	t
g	g	o	v	e	r	n	m	e	n	t	d	g	e	l	u	m	s
q	u	h	p	e	g	y	k	c	r	s	m	i	v	p	b	w	a
k	j	d	r	o	n	t	u	h	i	n	d	r	a	n	c	e	s

MODAL VERBS TO SHOW POSSIBILITY

Wallace is learning how modal verbs can help him understand how likely it is that something will happen. Always helpful when there's cheese and crackers to be eaten!

*We **will** eat cheese and crackers today.*

One use of a modal verb is to show how likely something is to happen. The most used modal verbs for possibility are:

might	will	must	shall	can	would	should

1

Wallace is trying to decide if the sentences are showing possibility or certainty. Help him by ticking the correct box for each sentence.

		Shows certainty	Shows possibility
a.	It might rain in West Wallaby Street tomorrow.		
b.	Wallace can eat a lot of cheese.		
c.	Wallace will have a cup of tea this afternoon.		
d.	Wallace may have an early night.		

Modal verbs can also be used to describe:

- **Ability** e.g. could succeed... can run if they want to...

- **Obligation** e.g. should be happy.... should be grateful... it would be rude not to...

- **Permission** e.g. can climb the tree because they have claws to grip.

2

Wallace needs to identify the modal verb in each sentence. Can you circle the modal verb for him?

a. In the football match, Wallace might score if he uses the Soccamatic invention.

b. Gromit was great at saving goals and Wallace knew that he should be pleased for him.

c. Wallace will be praised by the fans if he wins the cup.

d. After the game, they decided they would have a nice cuppa.

PREDICTING AND EXPLAINING

Christmas is coming! But what happens when the festive spirit gives way to the competitive spirit? Read the text below then answer the questions about it.

When the local paper announces its annual snowman-building competition, Gromit decides that this year he is going to be the winner. He spends hours delicately carving a splendid snow sculpture, which on closer inspection, bears a striking resemblance to his master...

Wallace arrives riding on his latest contraption, determined to win the competition too. The Snowman-O-Tron scoops up snow into its compacting compartment and out pops a ready-made snowman. Unfortunately, it ends up smashing Gromit's sculpture.

"Not bad for a first try," Wallace announces.

Gromit storms into the house, slamming the door behind him, dislodging a sheet of snow from the porch, completely covering Wallace. He's frozen to the spot — quite literally.

Gromit reaches for his camera and snaps his snow-covered master as his entry into the competition.

1

How did Gromit's attitude to Wallace change during the story? Tick one:

☐ He became more frustrated. ☐ He became more ashamed.

☐ He became more accepting. ☐ He became more competitive.

2

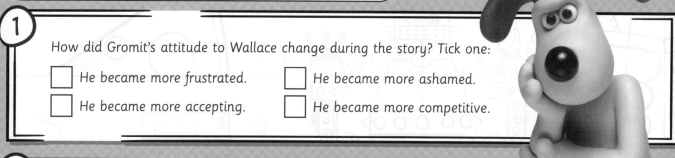

Can you use clues in the story to predict what might happen next and explain why you think this?

_____

_____

_____

_____

HYPHENS

Wallace is finding out more about hyphens!

Hyphens can join a prefix to a word and create compound words to make a sentence clearer. Although it looks like a dash, a hyphen is different; dashes join clauses while hyphens help create words.

1 Add the correct prefix **re-** or **co-** to the root words below.

a. _____ordinate	b _____enter	c. _____energise	d. _____operate
e. _____enact	f. _____elect	g. _____operation	h. _____equip

2 Can you explain how the hyphen helps make the meaning of the word clearer? Remember the prefix **re-** means again!

recover _____

re-cover _____

resign _____

re-sign _____

3 Can you add hyphens to join two or three words together so that the sentences make more sense?

a. When Wallace went to the moon, he came back empty handed.

_____

b. In the sky, Wallace saw twenty two shooting stars.

_____

c. The rocket should be finished now as Wallace used quick drying paint.

_____

WRITING A STORY FROM A PLAYSCRIPT

Wallace is thinking about the time he and Gromit got caught up in a murder mystery in A Matter of Loaf and Death.

Wallace knows that great dialogue has all the correct speech punctuation, uses a variety of words for 'said' and adds information about how it is said. e.g. "Get that thing away, lad" Wallace warned Gromit, as he runs away holding the bomb.

1 Help Wallace turn the script below into a story! Remember to make it dramatic by including lots of description with great adjectives to create atmosphere! Describe how Wallace is speaking and what Gromit is doing, to really show their characters. Continue your story on a separate piece of paper if you run out of room.

[Wallace is trying to light the candle on a cake. But his match won't strike.]
Wallace: Doh! Strike a light!
[Gromit is swinging towards the house on the end of a rope. From his point of view, we see the Wallace and Gromit house approaching fast! Gromit crashes through the window.]
Wallace: There you are! I think these matches are a bit...
[Gromit has zoomed across the table, grabbed a vase of flowers ... and when he comes to a stop the water pours out and soaks Wallace.]
Wallace: ... damp. Ah, yes, it's one of those joke candles, lad.
[The candle wants to go out, no matter how hard Gromit tries. He picks up the cake.]
Wallace: [shouting] Oi! Where are you going with that?
[Wallace trips up and flies in slow motion through the air.]
Wallace: ... CAAAAAAAAAKE!?
[Wallace lands on Gromit, the cake falls to the ground... and a bomb rolls out of it!]
Wallace: [shouting]! Gromit! It's a bomb! The cake's a bomb!
[Gromit looks to the heavens. He knew it was a bomb!]

-OUGH WORDS

Wallace is busy writing Christmas cards to his friends.

Wallace really wants to start perfecting his card-writing skills but is a little unsure about some words as they have different sounds. Words with **–ough** in are the ones he needs help with.

1

Match these unusual **-ough** words to their pictures.

bough

borough

dough

nought

plough

trough

a.

b.

c.

d.

e.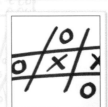

f.

2

There are seven sounds that **–ough** makes. Help Wallace sort the **–ough** words below into the sounds they make so he can choose the best words for his cards.

although   borough   bough   bought   brought   cough   dough   enough
fought   rough   thorough   though   thought   throughout   trough

off	oh	oo	or
		through	

ow	uff	uh
plough	tough	

30

ADVERBIALS

SCAN CODE

After Wallace's experience in A Matter of Loaf and Death, he is writing a journal about what happened.

One way to make paragraphs flow properly is by using adverbials at the start of sentences and paragraphs to help them connect to the next or the previous sentence or paragraph. Here are some examples of adverbials:

after a while	finally	nearby	one day	At the bottom of the hill

1

Wallace wants to add time and place adverbials to the beginning of his paragraphs but can't decide which ones to use. Can you choose either a time or a place adverbial for each paragraph and write it in? Remember to include a comma afterwards.

a. _____ Wallace and Gromit started a new bread baking business.

b. _____ they read in the paper about local bakers being killed by a bread-hating criminal figure.

c. _____ they see a pin-up girl for a bakery riding a bicycle with her poodle.

d. _____ the bike's breaks fail, and Wallace and Gromit try and save her.

e. _____ they manage to prevent the crash, and Wallace starts to fall in love!

2

Look at these adverbials. Can you use some of them to write three sentences about a fun day you've had?

firstly	later	then	subsequently	as a result	after
finally	however	at the same time	during	next	

_____

_____

_____

_____

ALPHABETICAL ORDER

Wallace has spent the whole day making some currant buns for his Top Bun bakery!

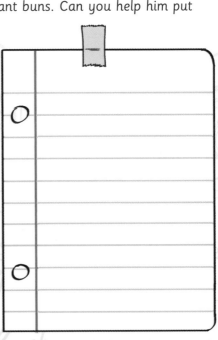

1 Wallace has written a list of the ingredients he needs for his currant buns. Can you help him put the list in alphabetical order?

Flour
Butter
Sugar
Yeast
Salt
Water
Currants
Jam

2 Wallace is looking for a better word for '**heat**' in the thesaurus to include in his currant bun recipe. He is currently on a page where the word at the top of the page is '**hole**'. Does he need to go **forwards** or **backwards** in the thesaurus to get to his word?

3 Wallace has written a list of cheese in alphabetical order, but Gromit thinks he has made a mistake. Can you rewrite the cheese names in the correct alphabetical order?

Stilton   Brie   Cheddar   Cottage   Gouda   Mozzarella   Parmesan   Emmental   Wensleydale   Cheshire

CREATIVE WRITING: WRITE A CHARACTER PROFILE

Wallace and Gromit are best friends and would do anything for each other. Wallace is able to describe Gromit's personality and his appearance by using descriptive phrases to help create a clear description.

1

Describe Gromit. Think about his looks and personality. Draw a picture of Gromit and write some ideas about how his personality might match or clash with Wallace.

Gromit:

_____

_____

_____

_____

Picture of Gromit:

2

Wallace has made a new friend at the cheese shop. He is trying to describe his new friend to Gromit using expanded noun phrases. He knows he needs to use two adjectives to describe the noun (e.g. long, dark hair) and can add more detail by adding a prepositional phrase at the end (e.g. long, dark hair with red highlights). Help him by picking three nouns and expanding them.

_____

_____

_____

3

Wallace is trying to describe his new friend to Wendolene. Can you write a character description using your expanded noun phrases to help him?

_____

_____

_____

SPELLINGS: -CIOUS OR -TIOUS

Wallace is busy planning out a brand-new invention. Before he can start making it, he wants to check his plans one more time.

> When adding the suffixes **-cious** or **-tious** to create adjectives, you need to see if the root word ends in **-ce** or **-cacy**. If it does, add **-cious** but if it doesn't, add **-tious**.

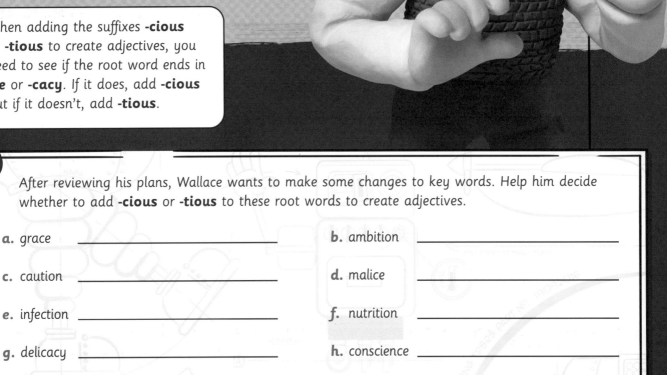

1

After reviewing his plans, Wallace wants to make some changes to key words. Help him decide whether to add **-cious** or **-tious** to these root words to create adjectives.

a. grace _____

b. ambition _____

c. caution _____

d. malice _____

e. infection _____

f. nutrition _____

g. delicacy _____

h. conscience _____

i. fiction _____

j. vice _____

2

Look at Wallace's spelling. Can you spot any spelling mistakes in using **-cious** or **-tious**? Tick if the spelling is correct and rewrite it correctly if he has made a mistake. Watch out for the exception to the rule which uses **-xious**!

a. spatious _____

b. nutricious _____

c. precious _____

d. suspitious _____

e. repetitious _____

f. ungracious _____

g. ancious _____

h. ferotious _____

USING COMMAS TO CLARIFY MEANING

Wallace always writes down his inventions when he's planning them. Because of this, he knows that a comma in the wrong place can sometimes lead to a very different meaning!

1

Look at the pairs of sentences. Help Wallace explain how the comma changes the meaning of the sentence.

a. Don't forget to call, Gromit!
Don't forget to call Gromit!

_____

b. Wallace's friends are Gromit his dog and Wendolene.
Wallace's friends are Gromit, his dog, and Wendolene.

_____

c. After leaving, Wendolene, Wallace and Gromit had a cup of tea.
After leaving Wendolene, Wallace and Gromit had a cup of tea.

_____

d. Cheese which comes from the moon is not nice to eat. It's delicious.
Cheese, which come from the moon, is not nice to eat. It's delicious.

_____

2

Wallace has written a shopping list to take to the village store but some of the commas are in the wrong place. Rewrite the list so that Wallace buys tea bags, Korn Flakes and dog shampoo.

Things to buy at the village store:
milk, tea, bags, cheese crackers, porridge, Korn, Flakes, dog, shampoo and oranges.

_____

_____

_____

_____

_____

Gromit wants nothing more than to be made employee of the month at Top Bun Bakery. To improve his chances, he's studying the employee handbook to make sure he knows what all of the words in it mean.

1

Help Gromit identify the different words and complete the crossword puzzle. The first letter has been given to you in the clues. Some of the other letters have been filled in to help you.

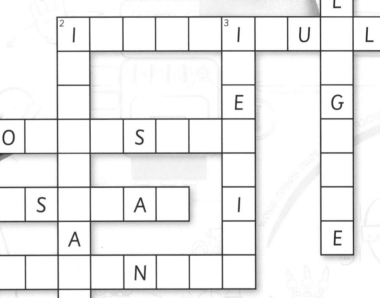

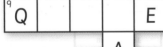

Across
2. A single person in a group. **(i)**
4. A paid job or occupation. **(p)**
5. Activity related to the body rather than the mind. **(p)**
6. A chance to make something possible. **(o)**
8. Extremely good or wonderful. **(m)**
9. A line of waiting people or vehicles. **(q)**

Down
1. Method of human communication through words or writing. **(l)**
2. When something happens instantly. **(i)**
3. The characteristics which make up a person. **(i)**
7. To make someone think or believe a certain thing. **(p)**

SCAN CODE

READING COMPREHENSION: INFERENCE PART 2

Wallace is writing a story about Feathers McGraw. He has tried hard to use detail to build up a picture in the readers mind when they read the story. He has also tried to include a variety of facts and opinions - opinions being what someone thinks is true while facts are literally facts!

Wallace needs to rent out the spare room in order to pay his bills. Enter Feathers McGraw: a notorious, villainous criminal with unnerving black eyes. This bird of many faces immediately uproots Gromit from his own bedroom, nabbing it for himself. Soon enough, his plotting drives poor Gromit out of the house. His endgame? To steal a diamond from the local museum with the help of Wallace's new invention: mechanical, robotic, walking trousers called 'Techno-Trousers', designed to take Gromit for walks.

Things start to take an even more sinister turn when Wallace wakes up for breakfast, only to find himself now wearing the Techno-Trousers that have been modified by Feathers. That evening, the small but nefarious villain makes a sleepwalking Wallace walk out of this house to the museum. Feathers uses the trouser's remote-control to make a sleeping Wallace steal a precious diamond.

Back at home, Feathers shuts Wallace and Gromit in a wardrobe. Fortunately, the pair manage to catch Feathers, take him to the police and give the diamond back to the museum. They are, however, unaware that Feathers is planning an escape to take his revenge...

1 What impression has Wallace given of Feathers McGraw? Find two adjectives that you feel describe Feathers and find evidence in Wallace's story that support your ideas.

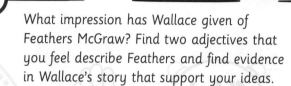

Impression	Evidence

2 Decide if these sentences are fact or whether they are Wallace's opinion. Tick the correct box.

		Fact	Opinion
a.	Feathers McGraw is a criminal.		
b.	He has black eyes.		
c.	He is a pitiless thief.		
d.	Feathers's aim is the steal the diamond.		

37

SPELLINGS: WORDS WITH SILENT LETTERS

Wallace uses words with silent letters a lot in his invention patterns. He has spotted several rules for knowing when a silent letter is used.

1 Help Wallace identify the silent letters in each word by circling them.

 doubt

 science

 scissors

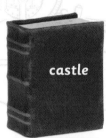 castle

 sign

 thumb

 knot

 walk

 column

 cupboard

 whistle

 island

 gnat

 write

 aisle

 ghost

2 Can you help Wallace complete his rules for silent letters?

a. Silent g or k is always before ___.

b. Silent n always comes after ___.

c. Silent ___ comes after w or g.

d. Silent s comes between ___ and ___.

e. Silent b comes either before ___ or after ___.

f. Silent ___ comes between s and l.

SYNONYMS AND ANTONYMS

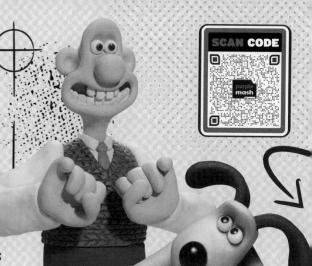

Wallace and Gromit know all too well about being similar and being opposite! Wallace is learning that synonyms are words that have the same or a very similar meaning while antonyms are pairs of words that are opposites.

1

Look at the words below and help Wallace to find four pairs of words that are synonyms and four pairs of words that are antonyms. The first ones have been done for you.

before	cold	sell	loud	hot	buy	peaceful
after	quiet	earlier	scorching	purchase		

SYNONYMS

before and earlier

_____

_____

_____

ANTONYMS

before and after

_____

_____

_____

2

Wallace is trying to think of some synonyms and antonyms for the words below. Can you help him find a suitable word for each?

Synonyms

big _____

small _____

fast _____

Antonyms

night _____

true _____

asleep _____

3

Wallace needs to find either a pair of antonyms or a pair of synonyms in each sentence. Can you underline the correct pair of words for them?

a. As the clock struck noon, Wallace and Gromit gathered for a midday cup of tea.

b. The valuable jewellery had all the stones stolen and became worthless.

c. Gromit cut the loaf of bread and sliced up the rolls.

CREATIVE WRITING: WRITING A POSTCARD IN ROLE

Wallace is writing a postcard to Wendolene on his travels to Blackpool. He knows that Wendolene will want lots of detail about what he is doing. He chooses to write informally so he can show how close they are.

1

Help Wallace change these phrases so that they're more informal.

Dear Wendolene, _____

I have been visiting a wide variety of tourist sights in Blackpool. _____

_____

It has been a fantastic holiday _____

_____

I cannot wait to see you again _____

2

Use the places that Wallace has visited to help him write another postcard to Wendolene. Remember to keep it informal but still use proper punctuation.

Things to see in Blackpool:
- **Blackpool Pleasure Beach**
- **The Tower Ballroom** • **Blackpool Zoo**
- **The Blackpool Tower**

Wendolene Ramsbottom

_____

_____

_____

_____

_____

_____

A20g

WALLACE
62 WEST WALLABY ST

HANDWRITING PRACTICE - PART 2

Wallace is writing a letter to Wendolene. He wants to make sure he presents his letter in his neatest handwriting.

1 Wallace is practising writing out sentences in his best handwriting. Write them out in the handwriting grids below, remembering to keep the words consistently sized and spaced.

I came up with a cracking contraption.

I had run out of crackers to go with the cheese.

2 Wallace wrote a paragraph about Gromit as quickly as he could. Look at what he came up with! How quickly can you copy it out neatly?

Gromit is a good lad. He has a good nature and a kind heart. He enjoys knitting, playing cards, reading the newspaper, building things and he does some cracking cooking.

USEFUL WORDS TO SPELL – PART 4

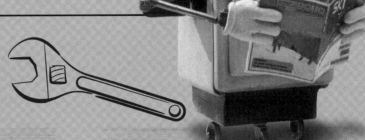

The Cooker is patrolling the Moon! In his efforts to protect it, he's muddled up the words that Wallace had been organising. Can you help him sort them out again?

1

Match the definition with the mixed-up word, then write the word correctly.
Each first letter has been given to you and the first match has been made for you.

a. A person's name written in a distinctive way. (s)

b. An organ in the body which plays a large role in digesting food. (s)

c. Something used to transport people or things across land. (v)

d. A large boat with sails. (y)

e. A person who serves in the army. (s)

f. The upper joint in a person's arm. (s)

g. A place where people can go to eat. (r)

ohsdurel _____

ehcvlie _____

unerstarat _____

isuerntga   signature   _____

ayhtc _____

lodsire _____

chtmaso _____

2

Help Wallace complete the spellings of these six words:

| rhythm | secretary | temperature | vegetable | rhyme | twelfth |

a. r _ _ _ _ m

b. r _ _ _ _

c. _ _ m _ _ _ _ _ _ _ e

d. v _ _ _ _ _ _ _ _

e. _ _ _ _ _ _ _ y

f. _ _ _ l _ _ _

ACTIVE AND PASSIVE SENTENCES

Wallace is writing some articles for the local paper. He's playing around with the order of words in his sentences to make them as strong as possible. To be able to do this, he needs to know what the subject and object is in each sentence. Then he can create active sentences – where the action is being done BY the subject – and passive sentences – where the action is being done TO the subject.

Feathers McGraw stole a diamond. This is an active sentence.

subject   object

A diamond was stolen by Feathers McGraw. This is a passive sentence.

1

Help Wallace to circle the subject and underline the object in each sentence.

a. Feathers McGraw stole a diamond.

b. The diamond was a priceless jewel.

c. The diamond landed in Wallace's helmet.

d. The Techno-Trousers set off the burglar alarm.

2

Wallace is turning his active sentences into passive sentences. He needs to change the order of the sentence, by swapping the **object** and the **subject**, and change the **verb**. He's finished the first sentence – can you complete the rest?

Active	Passive
a. The soccomatic throws balls.	Balls are thrown by the soccermatic.
b. The remote control gave a loud buzz.	_____ was given by _____.
c. The contraption makes a loud noise.	_____ is _____ by _____.
d. The porridge hit Preston in the face.	_____ was _____ in the face by _____.
e. Preston scares Wendolene.	_____.
f. Gromit put flowers in the garden.	_____.

BULLET POINTS AND NUMBERING

From how to make the Get-U-Up lever to how to invent the Knit-O-Matic, Wallace loves coming up with a plan! To help make his plans easier for Gromit to understand, he wants to learn how to use bullet points and numbering.

1

Wallce has a plan for making some Christmas cards. However, it is all in one long list! Can you separate the list into clear items and write each one against a bullet point?

Make a Christmas card machine, make a giant Robin costume, get some glitter, ask Gromit to wear the Robin costume, paint a fake scene on the curtains, take photos.

_____

_____

_____

_____

_____

_____

2

Wallace is trying to write instructions so he and Gromit can leave the house early but they're in the wrong order. Can you rewrite them in the correct order?

1. Set off together in the van.

2. Have a cracking cup of tea in bed.

3. Wake up nice and early with the alarm clock.

4. Make breakfast and pack the cheese and crackers.

5. Get everything loaded in the van.

_____

_____

_____

_____

_____

_____

_____

SEQUENCING AND SUMMARISING

Wallace is reminiscing about the time that he invented the Shopper 13! Read through the below and answer the questions.

Thursday

Deep beneath 62 West Wallaby Street, Wallace prepared to launch his latest invention. Wallace hit the ignition and, from underground, there emerged a remote-controlled shopping trolley which trundled forth.

With Wallace reading out directions from a map book, Gromit wrestled with a series of levers to guide the trolley towards its destination... the local Pick 'N' Save!

The trolley's built-in camera scanned the shelves until it found what Wallace was looking for – the biggest cheese in the store. But the weight of the giant Edam made one of the wheels come off the trolley. 'Gromit, we have a problem,' announced a worried Wallace.

The trolley spun around in lopsided circles until Gromit managed to make it grab a baguette which it used as a crutch to support itself.

As Wallace stared at his cheeseless crackers, Gromit followed the progress of the intrepid trolley on screen as it made its way home. Gromit managed to steer it through every obstacle and soon, Shopper 13 was ready to re-enter 62 West Wallaby Street. But at the last moment, tragedy struck! The other wheel came off the trolley and the giant Edam rolled back down the garden path.

'The Edam is stranded,' cried Wallace. 'We'll have to launch the probe.'

Right on cue, Shaun the Sheep shot out of a cat-flap in the garage door, riding on a skateboard. Unfortunately, the rescue mission failed to go to plan, as a horrified Wallace watched Shaun tuck into the tasty cheese feast!

1

Sequence these events in the order that they occurred. The first one has been done for you.

The trolley found the biggest cheese in the store.	
Shaun tucked into the tasty cheese feast.	
Wallace prepared to launch his latest invention.	1
Gromit managed to steer the trolley home.	
The wheel came off the trolley and the Edam rolled back down the garden path.	

2

A summary is a brief recollection of the key points of a text. Can you summarise Wallace's story in two sentences only?

_____

_____

ANSWERS

Page 2: Parts of a sentence

1. **noun**: d
   verb: f
   adjective: a
   adverb: g
   conjunction: c
   pronoun: h
   determiner: b
   preposition: e
2. **noun**: Wallace, trousers, friend, West Wallaby Street,
   verb: run, think, is
   adjective: clever, inventive
   adverb: quickly, suspiciously
   conjunction: because, and, as
   pronoun: him, he
   determiner: some, the
   preposition: under, near

Page 3: Linking ideas within a paragraph

1. The notes should be written into full sentences using the time conjunctions and adverbial phrases to join them together.

Page 4: Useful words to spell – Part 1

1. accommodate, according, accompany, aggressive, apparent, appreciate, attached, committee, communicate, community, correspond.

2.

```
w c c x l u z k a d a a s q c a i a
d o a n m x w m p i p c i c o y a k
l m c q d c a d p y p c k o r z g y
p m c p c j c a r s a o y m r r g r
c u o n m l c t e n r m q m e f r y
e n r y y l o t c i e m a u s m e e
x i d x b j m a i w n o f n p w s p
o c i i w d p c a s t d f i o x s q
t a n l h m a h t k s a u t n u i w
r t g k c s n e e a x t i y d c v x
v e a i o r y d y w z e f x i t e b
g z t a u f b a c o m m i t t e e s
```

Page 5: Commas, brackets and dashes

1. a. also known as the sweet spot
   b. the expert baker
   c. the rival bakery owner
   d. the pampered pooch
   e. the handsome inventor
2. Brackets, commas and dashes can be used to mark all sentences.

Page 6: Speedy reading

1. a. False   c. False   e. True
   b. True   d. True
2. Because it was the cup final and the two teams were fierce rivals.

Page 7: Adding suffixes to create verbs

1. a. horror - horrify
   b. threat - threaten
   c. fright - frighten
   d. terror - terrify or terrorise
   e. energy - energise
   f. irritation - irritate
   g. terror
2. **beautiful** - beautify
   character - characterise
   hard - harden
   active - activate
   electric - electrify
   light - lighten
   regular - regulate
   equal - equalise

Page 8: Suffixes -able and -ably

1. a. adorable   e. favourably
   b. considerable   f. enjoyable
   c. dependable   g. reliable
   d. responsible   h. knowledgeable
2. a. changeable   c. noticeable
   b. manageable

Page 9: Making an account flow across paragraphs

1. Three paragraphs should have been written telling the story. Each paragraph should finish on an ellipsis and have key words and phrases repeating through them.

Page 10: Semicolons, colons and dashes

1. a. Cheddar cheese is made in the village of Cheddar**:** It's one of Wallace's favourite cheeses!
   b. Wallace visited Cheddar on a cheese pilgrimage**:** He had to go there as he had run out of supplies.
2. Wallace drove out of town**;** he was in search of much needed crackers.
3. In the end, Wallace stayed in town and opened a cheese shop - gaining the respect of the community - where his cheese was loved by many.

Page 11: Reading comprehension: inference - Part 1

1. a. The hushed sounds of the pages turning.
   b. He was amazed by what he sees.
2. a. Dimly lit bulb
   b. Wallace feels shocked or surprised as he gasps and his eyes widen.

Page 12: Adding prefixes

1. **mis**behaves, **dis**agrees, **dis**approve, **dis**obedience, **over**reaction, **re**view, **re**acted, **dis**respectful, **un**comfortable
2. a. **over**take   d. **over**look
   b. **re**build   e. **re**charge
   c. **re**write   f. **re**make

Page 13: Spellings: Ei words – Part 1

2. a. prot**ei**n   d. f**ie**ld
   b. shr**ie**k   e. caff**ei**ne
   c. s**ei**ze   f. th**ie**f

Page 14: Writing a playscript

1. The playscript should have a new line for each speaker with stage directions written in brackets.

Page 15: Writing a newspaper report

1. The finished piece of writing should contain all the information outlined on the page and include an introduction, main paragraph and conclusion.

Page 16: Relative clauses

1. a. where   c. which/that
   b. whose   d. which/that
2. Any variations using relative pronouns to describe the bold word are acceptable, they do not have to rhyme.

Page 17: Spellings: ei words - Part 2

1. a. ✔   e. ✗ thief
   b. ✗ receive   f. ✔
   c. ✗ neighbour g. ✗ receipt
   d. ✔   h. ✔
2. science: b   ancient: c
   sufficient: c species: c
   juicier: d   society: b
   conscience: c iciest: d

Page 18: Colons and semicolons in lists

1. a. Things Gromit needs: wire, screwdriver, paint.
   b. Items to source: wood, nails, saw, bicarbonate of soda.
   c. The days I can submit my project: Monday, Tuesday, Wednesday, Thursday, Friday.

2. To get the winning prize and not crash, I need to: fill the fuel tank with enough fuel to fly for a long distance and fast; show the other pilots that I have won many other competitions to scare them, even though I have only won two; put cheese in the other planes jets to make them spin slower; get Wallace to hack the other planes to do their tricks wrong; do five loop-the-loops.

Page 19: Reading comprehension: vocabulary

1. a. Sourcing
   b. Small increments or temperature changes.
   c. Similar

2. Straight away

3. Conversely means the opposite, the reverse.

Page 20: Adverbs to indicate possibility

1. **Certain or very likely:** certainly, definitely, clearly, obviously
   Might: maybe, possibly, perhaps, probably

2. a. clearly   c. perhaps
   b. definitely   d. possibly

Page 21: Spellings: homophones

1. **Noun:** advice, device, licence, practice, prophecy
   Verb: advise, devise, license, practise, prophesy
   a. advice, advise   c. practice, practise
   b. devise, device

2. **stationary:** not moving.
   stationery: paper, envelopes etc
   desert: to abandon, a barren place
   dessert: a sweet course after the main course of a meal.
   compliment: to make nice remarks about someone
   complement: to make something complete or more complete
   ascent: going up
   assent: agreement, to agree

Page 22: Handwriting Practice 1

Handwriting should be joined, even and consistently sized and spaced.

Page 23: Creative writing: Writing a plot

The plot can be written in either present or past tense but should be written in full sentences and punctuated accurately.

Page 24: Verb tenses

1. a. Wallace has read the inventor magazine.
   b. Gromit has fixed a broken invention.
   c. Piella has waited for the bread to be baked.
   d. Wendolene has walked into the wool shop.
   e. Preston has eaten a bowl of dog food.

2. a. Gromit had walked down the stairs.
   b. He had noticed my invention.
   c. He had tripped on it anyway.
   d. He had landed in a pile of wires.
   e. Gromit had tidied everything away neatly.

Page 25: Useful words to spell – Part 2

1.

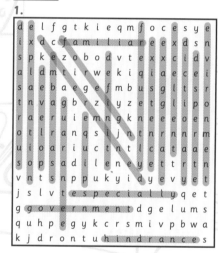

Page 26: Modal verbs to show possibility

1. a. Shows possibility
   b. Shows certainty
   c. Shows certainty
   d. Shows possibility

2. a. might   c. will
   b. should   d. would

Page 27: Predicting and explaining

1. He became more frustrated.

2. Answers could include: Gromit's entry could or could not win, Wallace could shake himself free to create a new snowman using the Snowman-O-Tron, in which case Gromit might become even more frustrated.

Page 28: Hyphens

1. a. **co**-ordinate   e. **re**-enact
   b. **re**-enter   f. **re**-elect
   c. **re**-energise   g. **co**-operation
   d. **co**-operate   h. **re**-equip

2. **recover:** This means to get better after something
   re-cover: This means to cover again
   resign: This means to quit your job
   re-sign: This means to sign again

3. a. empty-handed
   b. twenty-two
   c. quick-drying

Page 29: Writing a story from a playscript

1. The story should be in past tense and include a range of description in between the speech.

Page 30: -ough words

1. a. plough   d. trough
   b. borough   e. nought
   c. bough   f. dough

2. **off:** cough, trough
   oh: although, dough, though
   oh: through, throughout
   or: bought, brought, fought, thought
   ow: plough, bough
   uff: tough, enough, rough
   uh: borough, thorough

Page 31: Adverbials

1. a. One day,
   b. After a while,
   c. Nearby,
   d. At the bottom of the hill,
   e. Finally,

2. Sentences should include some of the suggested words to describe a day.

Page 32: Alphabetical order

1. butter, currants, flour, jam, salt, sugar, water, yeast

2. backwards

3. Brie, Cheddar, Cheshire, Cottage, Emmental, Gouda, Mozzarella, Parmesan, Stilton, Wensleydale

Page 33: Creative writing: write a character profile

1. Multiple ideas correct.

2. Three expanded noun phrases should be written.

3. Character description needs to include the three expanded noun phrases planned and be written in full sentences.

Page 34: Spellings: -cious or -tious

1. a. gracious
   b. ambitious
   c. cautious
   d. malicious
   e. infectious
   f. nutritious
   g. delicious
   h. conscious
   i. fictitious
   j. vicious

2. a. spacious
   b. nutritious
   c. ✔
   d. suspicious
   e. ✔
   f. ✔
   g. anxious
   h. ferocious

Page 35: Using commas to clarify meaning

1. a. The first sentence is telling Gromit to call and the second tells you to call for Gromit.
   b. The first sentence makes it sound like Gromit and Wendolene are his friends and the second sounds like Gromit, his dog and Wendolene are his friends.
   c. The first sentence shows all three are having a cup of tea and the second only Wallace and Gromit are.
   d. The first sentence makes it sound like cheese which comes from the moon is not nice and in the second it is extra information that it comes from the moon.

2. Things to buy at the Village Store: milk, teabags, cheese, crackers, porridge, Korn Flakes, dog shampoo and oranges.

Page 36: Useful words to spell – Part 3

1. **Across:**
   2. individual
   4. profession
   5. physical
   6. opportunity
   8. marvellous
   9. queue
   Down:
   1. language
   2. immediately
   3. identity
   7. persuade

Page 37: Reading comprehension: inference - Part 2

1. **Impression:** evil
   Evidence: Villainous criminal, unnerving black eyes.

   Impression: Cunning
   Evidence: Bird of many faces, plotting, sinister turn.

2. a. Fact
   b. Fact
   c. Opinion
   d. Fact

Page 38: Spellings: Words with silent letters

1. doubt, science, scissors, castle, sign, thumb, knot, walk, column, cupboard, whistle, island, gnat, write, aisle, ghost.

2. a. n
   b. m
   c. h
   d. i and l
   e. t or after m
   f. t

Page 39: Synonyms and antonyms

1. **Synonyns**
   before and earlier
   hot and scorching
   buy and purchase
   quiet and peaceful

   Antonym
   before and after <u>or</u> earlier and after
   hot and cold <u>or</u> scorching and cold
   buy and sell <u>or</u> purchase and sell
   quiet and loud <u>or</u> peaceful and loud

2. **Synonyms**
   big <u>e.g. large</u>
   small <u>e.g. tiny</u>
   fast <u>e.g. speedy</u>
   Antonyms
   night <u>e.g. day</u>
   true <u>e.g. false</u>
   asleep <u>e.g. awake</u>

3. a. <u>noon</u>, <u>midday</u>
   b. <u>valuable</u>, <u>worthless</u>
   c. <u>cut</u>, <u>sliced</u>

Page 40: Creative writing: writing a postcard in role

1. **For example:**
   Hi Wendolene.
   I've been to loads of tourist spots. It's been a cracking holiday. Can't wait to see you soon, chuck!

2. **For example:**
   Postcard should be written informally as per question 1.

Page 41: Handwriting practice 2

Handwriting should be joined, even and consistently sized and spaced.

Page 42: Useful words to spell – Part 4

1. a. signature
   b. stomach
   c. vehicle
   d. yacht
   e. solider
   f. shoulder
   g. restaurant

2. a. rhythm
   b. rhyme
   c. temperature
   d. vegetable
   e. secretary
   f. twelfth

Page 43: Active and passive sentences

1. a. (Feathers McGraw) <u>a diamond</u>.
   b. (The diamond) <u>priceless jewel</u>.
   c. (The diamond) <u>Wallace's helmet</u>.
   d. (The Techno-Trousers) <u>burglar alarm.</u>

2. **Passive**
   a. Balls are thrown by the soccermatic.
   b. A loud buzz was given by the remote control.
   c. A loud noise is made by the contraption.
   d. Preston was hit in the face by the porridge.
   e. Wendolene is scared by Preston.
   f. Flowers were put in the garden by Gromit.

Page 44: Bullet points and numbering

1. • Make a Christmas card machine,
   • Make a giant Robin costume,
   • Get some glitter,
   • Ask Gromit to wear the Robin costume,
   • Paint a fake scene on the curtains,
   • Take photos.

2. 1. Wake up nice and early with the alarm clock.
   2. Have a cracking cup of tea in bed.
   3. Make breakfast and pack the cheese and crackers.
   4. Get everything loaded in the van.
   5. Set off together in the van.

Page 45: Sequencing and Summarising

1. 2, 5, 1, 4, 3

2. Accept any two sentences which summarise the main events of Wallace's story. For example:

   Wallace created an invention to do his cheese shopping.

   The invention was useless as the wheels fell off and Wallace didn't get his cheese.